PANDORA'S BOX

Retold by MARY POPE OSBORNE

Pictures by LISA AMOROSO

SCHOLASTIC INC.

New York Toronto London Auckland Sydney

ISBN 0-590-40767-8

12 11 10 9 8 7 6 5 4 3 2 1   7 8 9/8 0 1 2/9

Printed in the U.S.A.   08

First Scholastic printing, October 1987

For Susan
—M. P.O.

For Donna and Gary
—L. A.

About this story

This story has been told for hundreds of years. It comes from the country of Greece.

In the days hundreds and hundreds of years ago, the Greek people believed in many different gods. Each one had a personality and certain special powers. The people believed that these gods caused everything that happened on Earth: They made the rain fall and the crops grow. They caused volcanoes, floods, and earthquakes.

The Greeks made up many stories about their gods. They said the gods lived on top of a mountain called Mount Olympus. The stories about the gods of Mount Olympus and other gods are known as the Greek myths.

Pandora's Box is one Greek myth. At one time, the story goes, there were no women on Earth. So Zeus, the ruler of Mount Olympus, told the blacksmith god to make a woman out of clay. The blacksmith god made the first woman and named her Pandora.

The gods gave Pandora gifts to take with her to Earth. One gave her beauty. One gave her music. Another gave her the craft of weaving. Another gave her curiosity. And Zeus gave Pandora a golden box—but he told her she must never open it.

Then Hermes, the messenger god, took Pandora down from Mount Olympus and led her to Earth. At that time Earth was a very happy place without any troubles or sorrows. . . .

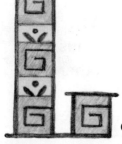ong ago there lived on Earth
a man named Epimetheus.
He lived alone in the country near the sea.
One day Epimetheus heard a knock on his door.
He opened it and saw a lovely maiden standing
before him. Epimetheus had never seen anyone
like her before!
She had flowers in her hair.
She wore a long robe of fine cloth.
She held a small harp and a golden box.

"My name is Pandora," she said.
"May I come in?
The god Zeus sent me to be your wife."

Epimetheus had once been warned by
his brother, Prometheus, never to accept
any gifts from Zeus.
But Epimetheus could not turn Pandora away.
She was the first woman on Earth.

"Yes, you may come in!" he said.

Pandora brought her harp
and golden box into the house.

"What is in the golden box?"
Epimetheus asked her.

"I do not know," she said. "Zeus gave it to me.
But he told me *never* to open it."

"Well then, I suppose you should not,"
said Epimetheus.

"Yes, I suppose not," said Pandora.

And so Pandora and Epimetheus
began a happy life together.

There were no troubles on Earth at that time.
Pandora spent her days baking and weaving

and playing her harp.

She liked to run in the fields
and swim in the ocean.
She was curious about everything on Earth:
the plants and animals, the birds and trees.

She was also very curious about the golden box.
Often she took it out from underneath her bed
and held it up to the light
and turned it around.

"Are you looking at that box again?"
Epimetheus asked her one day.

"Yes," said Pandora. "Do you think
I could take a little peek inside?"

"No, Zeus told you not to," said Epimetheus.

Pandora sighed. "I suppose you are right,"
she said. "I will put it out of sight—
someplace I never go."

So Pandora hid the golden box
in the wine cellar.

But every day she went to the wine cellar
to look at the golden box.

"Are you looking at that box again?"
Epimetheus asked one day.

"Yes," sighed Pandora. "I am so curious
to know what is in it!
Maybe it is full of silver or gold!"

"But Zeus told you *never* to open it, remember?"
Epimetheus said. "Perhaps you should take it
out of the house and put it someplace far away."

"I suppose I should," said Pandora.

So Pandora carried the golden box
down to the sea, and she buried it
deep in a cave near the water.

"That should do it," she said.

But late that night Pandora woke up.
She thought she heard voices telling her
to hurry to the sea cave and open the golden box.
She thought she could feel invisible hands
pulling her from her bed.

Pandora got up and crept out of the house.
She carried a lantern down to the cave near the sea,
and she dug up the golden box.
She was just about to open it—
when Epimetheus yelled, "Stop!"

"I heard you get up, and I followed you!"
he said. "I think you need to put the box
in a new hiding place."

And so, in the rosy dawn,
Pandora carried the golden box back home.
She put the box inside a large storage jar.
Then she put the storage jar inside an old chest.
She tied a rope around the chest
and then put the chest down, down,
deep into an empty well in the garden.

"Dear me," she said. "Surely that will do it now!"

From then on, Pandora tried very hard
to forget about the box.
She planted her garden and played her harp.
She took care of the animals
and swam in the sea.

But one rainy spring day,
when her husband was away from home,
Pandora found herself feeling *very* curious
about the golden box.

"I wonder if it is still there," she said.

It was raining hard as Pandora went outside.
Lightning flashed and thunder cracked in the sky.
Pandora pulled on the rope
that hung outside the empty well.
Up came the chest.
Pandora pushed the chest along the wet grass
to a covered courtyard.

She took the storage jar out of the old chest.
Then she took the golden box
out of the storage jar.
The rain came down harder than ever
as Pandora held the golden box in her hands.
It gleamed in the misty stormlight.

She thought she heard the box say, "Open me!"

"No, I must not!" she yelled.

She started to put the golden box back
into the storage jar—but then she stopped.

"Maybe I will just take a quick peek,"
she said. "And then I will not be curious
about it anymore."

Pandora held her breath
as she gently lifted the lid of the box.
Out flew a creature—
a horrible ugly thing with wings.
Pandora cried out and dropped the box.
More ugly creatures flew out,
squealing and screeching and flapping their wings.
They flew around Pandora's head,
calling out their names:
Envy! Greed! Meanness!
Rudeness! Hate! Spite!

Pandora covered her head with her hands.
The creatures flapped their wings some more.
Then they flew out of the courtyard
and into the world.

"Oh, what have I done?" Pandora said.
She began to cry.

"Wait! Look! Look at me!"
A tiny voice came from inside the box.

"Oh, please, please, leave me alone,"
said Pandora.

"Look at me," the voice said again.

Slowly Pandora picked up the box.
She lifted the lid.

There was one creature left inside.
This creature was not ugly.
It had a beautiful face,
and a golden light shone about it.

"Stop crying," squeaked the little creature.
"I will help you and others
    if you take care of me
    and do not let the other creatures kill me."

Pandora stopped crying and gently lifted
the shining creature out of the box.
"What is your name?" she asked.

The creature answered, "I am Hope."

Pandora hugged Hope to her heart.

From then on, life on Earth was different.
People were no longer always happy
and carefree.
They now had bad feelings as well—
feelings brought by the ugly winged creatures.
But there was always Hope,
and Hope helped protect people from the evils
that had flown out of Pandora's box.

Note to Readers

You might want to know more about the twelve gods of Mount Olympus.

Zeus—(say *zoose*) god of the sky, father god. He gave Pandora the golden box.

Hera—(say *HAIR-a*) wife of Zeus, goddess of marriage. She gave Pandora the gift of curiosity.

Hephaestus—(say *hee-FAY-stus*) son of Hera, blacksmith god. He made Pandora out of clay.

Aphrodite—(say *af-ro-DYE-tee*) goddess of love and beauty. She gave Pandora the gift of beauty.

Apollo—(say *a-POL-lo*) son of Zeus, god of the sun, god of music and beauty. He gave Pandora the gift of music.

Athena—(say *a-THEE-na*) daughter of Zeus, goddess of war, goddess of city and crafts, goddess of wisdom. She gave Pandora the gift of weaving.

Hermes—(say *HER-mees*) son of Zeus, messenger god. He took Pandora to Earth.

Ares—(say *AIR-ees*) son of Zeus, god of war.

Artemis—(say *AR-te-miss*) Apollo's twin sister, goddess of the hunt.

Poseidon—(say *po-SIGH-don*) Zeus's brother, god of the sea.

Hades—(say *HAY-dees*) Zeus's brother, god of the underworld, god of the dead.

Hestia—(say *HES-ti-a*) Zeus's sister, goddess of the hearth.

Prometheus—(say *pro-MEE-thee-us*) Another name you read in this story is Prometheus. He was the brother of Pandora's husband, Epimetheus (say *ep-ih-MEE-thee-us*). Prometheus was a Titan, a group of gods older than the gods of Mount Olympus. Prometheus was known as the creator of man and man's best friend. He made Zeus angry by stealing fire from the gods and giving it to man. That is why Zeus sent Pandora's box down to Earth—to punish man for accepting fire from Prometheus.